A DUMMY'S GUIDE:

# HOW TO USE VIVEZA 2, NIK SOFTWARE

Jonathan Curtis

Copyright © 2013 Regent Publishing

All rights reserved.

ISBN-13: 978-1493729340

# DISCLAIMER

All contents copyrighted © 2013 Jonathan Curtis and Regent Publishing. All rights reserved worldwide. No part of this document or the related materials may be reproduced or transmitted in any form, by any means (electronic, photocopying, recording, or otherwise) without the prior permission by the author/ publisher.

The service and the materials contained within *A Dummy's Guide: How To Use Viveza 2, Nik Software* are based on the author's experience of using the software and working as a professional photographer. The information provided in this book is not a substitute for professional advice.

In no event shall the author be liable for any direct, indirect, incidental, punitive, or consequential damages of any kind whatsoever with respect to the service, the materials and the products contained within.

# TABLE OF CONTENTS

Disclaimer ........................................................................... 3

Introduction ....................................................................... 9
   Benefits of Using Viveza ...................................................... 10
   When You Should Not Use Viveza ........................................ 12
   What's New in Viveza 2? ..................................................... 15
      *Global Adjustments ................................................... 16*
      *Structure Enhancement ............................................ 17*
      *Levels and Curves ..................................................... 17*
      *Shadow Adjustment Enhancement .......................... 18*
      *Control Point Response ............................................. 19*
      *Improved Interface ................................................... 19*
      *Undo & Redo ............................................................. 20*
      *Selection Engine ........................................................ 20*
   Viveza 2 vs. Other Photo Editing Plug-ins ........................... 21
   What is U Point Technology? ............................................... 22

Getting Started ................................................................ 25
   How to Install ....................................................................... 25
      *Installation on Mac .................................................... 26*
      *Installation on Windows ............................................ 28*

Viveza Lightroom ..................................................................29
    *Using Viveza with Photoshop* ....................................................*32*
    *Using Viveza with Aperture* ......................................................*33*
Viveza Interface ..................................................................34
    *View Modes*..............................................................................*35*
    *Image Area*..............................................................................*36*
    *Loupe & Navigation*.................................................................*37*
    *Controls Panel* .........................................................................*39*
    *Tools* .........................................................................................*40*
Viveza Control ....................................................................41
    *Levels & Curves* .......................................................................*43*
    *Structure*..................................................................................*44*
    *Hue*..........................................................................................*45*

**Viveza Global Adjustments ..................................... 47**
Local Adjustments ..............................................................47
How Global Adjustments Work ..........................................48
What You Can Adjust..........................................................48
How to Use Global Adjustments ........................................50

**Viveza Selections .................................................... 53**
Selecting Complex Objects .................................................53
Selecting Areas with Control Points ..................................54
    *Photoshop Tools* ......................................................................*54*
    *Lightroom Edge Detection*.......................................................*55*
    *Color Range* .............................................................................*55*
    *From Viveza Interface*..............................................................*55*
Adding a Control Point ......................................................56
Using Control Points ..........................................................57
Managing Control Points...................................................58
    *Show/Hide Checkbox (Effects)*..................................................*59*

    *Control Point Numbers* ............................................................... *59*
    *Percentage of Area Covered* ....................................................... *59*
    *Selection Masks* .......................................................................... *60*
    *Delete & Duplicate* ..................................................................... *60*
  Grouping a Control Point ............................................................ 61
    *Why Group Control Points?* ........................................................ *61*
    *Creating a Group* ........................................................................ *63*
    *Using the Group* ......................................................................... *64*
    *Deleting a Group or Ungrouping Control Points* ....................... *65*

**Changing the Color of the Selected Areas** ............................ **67**
    *Using the Color Picker* ................................................................ *69*
    *Using the Eye Dropper* ................................................................ *69*

**Viveza Adjustments** ................................................................ **71**
  Brightness ...................................................................................72
  Contrast ......................................................................................73
  Saturation ...................................................................................74
  Red, Green & Blue (RGB) ............................................................74
  Structure .....................................................................................75
  Shadows .....................................................................................77
  Warmth ......................................................................................77
  Hue ..............................................................................................78
  Levels & Curves ..........................................................................79

**Keyboard Shortcuts** ................................................................ **83**
  Keyboard Shortcuts for Windows ..............................................83
  Keyboard Shortcuts for Mac .......................................................84

**Examples** ................................................................................. **87**
  Making the Sky Darker ...............................................................87
  Improving Contrast & Color ........................................................90

**Expert Tips ........................................................................ 93**
  Selecting the Adjustments ...................................................93
  Saving Money on Buying Viveza 2 .......................................95
  Follow the Installation Wizard..............................................95
  Using Levels & Curves ...........................................................96
**Conclusion............................................................................ 99**

# INTRODUCTION

With all the tools available to photographers today, one would assume they have the resources they need to enhance the quality of the pictures they take. What could new software possibly have to offer? This is where Viveza comes in. Launched by Nik Software in 2008, Viveza has taken color and light adjustment in pictures to the next level.

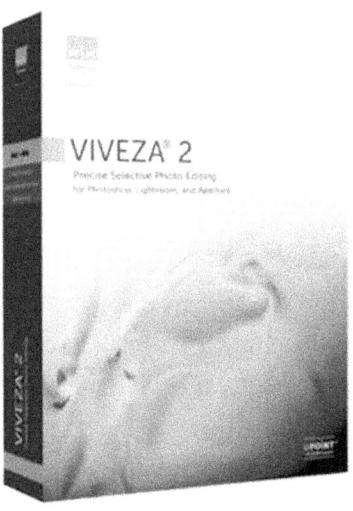

Even the most complicated and complex changes to the pictures you take can be made with ease using Viveza. This is made possible by the inclusion of U Point technology. Before Viveza, this technology was only available in the Nikon Capture NX. The photo editing program by Nikon restricted its use as it was designed mainly for Nikon cameras.

Viveza, on the other hand, is made for all brands and types of cameras professional photographers use. Nik Software recently released Viveza 2.0, a significant improvement on the original software. The great thing is that the software retains its ease of use and simplicity while enhancing the range of features available to you, the end user.

The basic premise of the software is the same and you can extract the same purpose from it as you did from the original Viveza. So, if you are looking for a program that will help you change the color or light levels of the images you capture on your camera, Viveza is the perfect choice.

This book is intended as a guide for using Viveza. From downloading the software to learning to use it, this book offers all the information you require about this top-of-the-line photography software. Read on till the end and you will be able to master the use of Viveza. Best of luck!

To start things off, we will look at the various benefits of using Viveza. Only then will it become clear to you why you should opt for this software over any other available on the market.

## Benefits of Using Viveza

Viveza can be used with other leading photography software to enhance picture quality. If you are familiar with Aperture or Photoshop, you can add Viveza 2.0 as a plug-in to either. This gives you greater control over the final images you produce and deliver to your customers. You can get over the limitations of conventional and popular photo editing programs by using Viveza in combination with them.

Introduction

The main feature of Viveza is the U Point. When using Photoshop or any other program for adjusting the colors in an image, you have to get through all the different layers. This not only increases the time and effort you have to invest but also increases the chances of error. One slip and you could ruin the picture. Though the errors can be undone, it is possible you might overlook some important aspects.

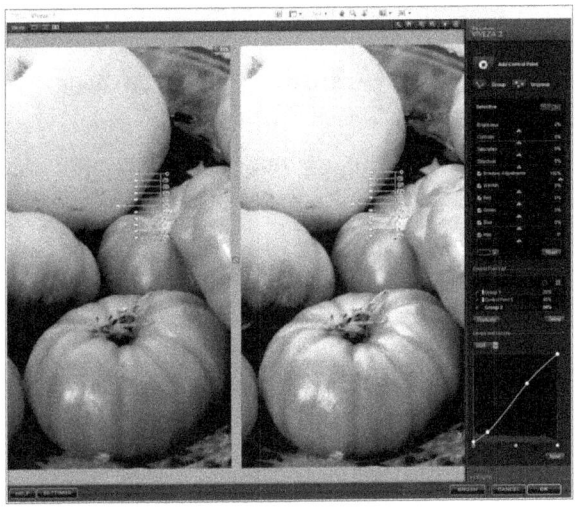

Instead of having to adjust all the layers, you can simply place a U Point on the part of the image you want to change. You can set the values for light and color in the selected area. The values you enter will be rendered on the images and you can see the effects. There are no restrictions on the area you can select for adjustment. You can even change the color of the entire picture using Viveza.

Also, there are a range of changes you can make to the picture. These include adjusting the brightness and/or contrast, hue and saturation. The software also gives you the option of adjusting individual colors in the picture. You have greater control over the end product and get the picture to look exactly the way you want. We will examine each of these changes in more detail in the coming chapters.

What's more, with Viveza 2.0, you have the luxury of selecting different parts of a picture and then combining them to form one image. Even if you don't want to combine the images, you can still use the multiple selection option to adjust the color and light of the picture. The changes are made in sync, making it easier for you to carry them out. If you don't feel this feature is working out for you, you can always select individual parts and adjust their appearance.

Plus, you don't have to work too hard to learn how to use Viveza. Reading through this book from cover to cover will ensure that you have the required information and knowledge needed to make the most of this software. Only then can you make the most of what it has to offer.

## When You Should Not Use Viveza

Regardless of the fact that there are numerous benefits of using Viveza 2.0 over other photo editing plug-ins on the market, there are some instances where using it is not the best option for you. This doesn't at all mean that there are any drawbacks to using Viveza 2.0. It is just that it needs certain software to work with and can only be used for some specific purposes.

Introduction

Here is a list of instances when you should not use Viveza.

- If you are working with monochrome images, Viveza 2.0 won't be of much use to you. The plug-in hasn't been designed to work on monochromic images, so keep that in mind.
- Sometimes all you need is to airbrush certain parts of an image to improve its quality. In that case, using Viveza 2.0 will only complicate matters for you. There is no doubt that Viveza is a great software and has all the features a professional photographer could need for editing his/her images but if a brush can do the job, use a brush.
- If you don't have Photoshop Smart Objects, don't even think of using Viveza 2.0. The reason for this is quite simple: you won't be able to save the changes you make to the images using the plug-in. In other words, the changes will prove to be destructive. You won't be able to recover the change you've made to the image, including any Control Points you may have added.
- Lastly, Viveza has been designed to edit complex objects but it can only help you make local changes. If you want to make global adjustments to your pictures, you will have to use other software. This can be termed a shortcoming of the software but it is more of a missing feature.

So, these are the different situations and instances in which using Viveza will not prove to be the best option for you. On the flip side, if you fulfill all the requirements as outlined in the list above, you can use the plug-in to edit the images you have taken.

## How to Use Viveza 2

Then you will find there are few better options available to you than Viveza 2.0.

Apart from the points listed above, there is one more function for which Viveza 2 is not the best plug-in to use, i.e. when you are processing a batch of images at the same time. This doesn't at all mean that Viveza 2 cannot be used for batch processing. However, it isn't the best program for batch processing. The features and settings available to you make it ill-suited for batch processing.

So, even though you can easily batch process using Viveza 2, it is better that you don't. The main reason for this is the design of the Control Points. They are specific to the location they are placed on. Whenever you perform an action or adjust a setting, the position of the Control Point cannot be changed after that. You have to undo the change as well as remove the Control Point to be able to process the batch perfectly.

This is quite a hassle for you to bear. Given the fact that there are better photo editing programs that have the features required for batch processing, you should avoid using Viveza 2 for this purpose. Another reason for this is that in most images, the location of a certain object or subject would change. This will make it next to impossible for you to apply the same changes to all the images.

Even if you do render the changes to each image in a batch, the difference in location from one image to the next will mean you cannot achieve the desired result. This means that the only situation in which you can use Viveza 2 for batch processing is if you have taken the images using a tripod or are processing a batch of still life images.

Introduction

In all other cases, you won't be able to achieve the results you are looking for if you process a batch of images using Viveza 2.

As you can see, the features and specifications of Viveza are superior to most of the photo editing software being used by professional photographers today. At the same time, you have to remember the situations in which Viveza 2.0 is not the best plug-in to use.

You can purchase the Viveza 2 plug-in for $199.95. If you have the original Viveza installed on your computer or mobile device, you can upgrade it to the second generation program for just $99.95. The price is justified as the plug-in offers superior quality and a host of new features.

## What's New in Viveza 2?

Nik Software has released a new version of its photo editing plug-in Viveza. Photographers familiar with the Viveza plug-in will find Viveza 2.0 easy to use. If you have used Viveza, using the new version becomes much simpler. This book will provide the information you need to get familiar with the plug-in.

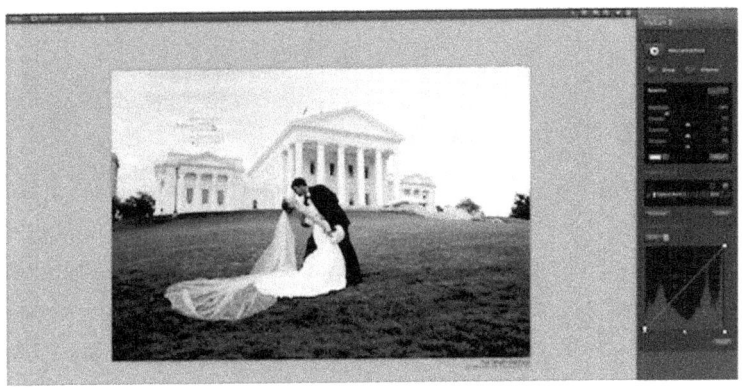

How to Use Viveza 2

Though the interface and other features of the plug-in are the same, there are a number of new settings and controls that have been added to it. This is why you need to familiarize yourself with Viveza 2 before you begin using it. Before moving on to the main part of the book, it is important that the new features of the plug-in be highlighted.

Here is a list of the new features that you will find in Viveza 2:

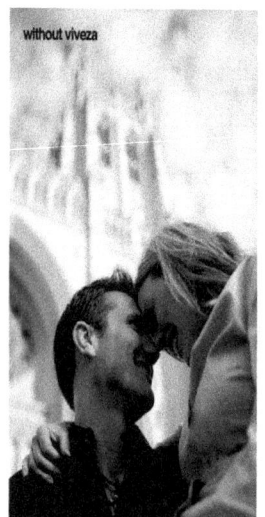
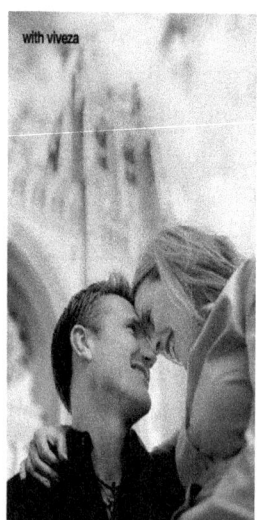

## *Global Adjustments*

Through Global Adjustments, you have the option to make changes to the entire image. You can place Control Points and then render changes to different parts of the image. Though Viveza has been designed to provide photographers the chance to edit different parts of the image, Global Adjustments enable you to modify the entire image.

Introduction

If you want to make some changes to an image, you can easily do so through the Global Controls. You can adjust the color, tone or style to ensure that there is cohesion among different parts of the image. This gives you greater control over the editing process.

## Structure Enhancement

You can enhance the details of the structures in your pictures using the new Structure Enhancement. There is a slider available to adjust the level of detailing. This not only allows you to make structures appear smoother but also remove the effects brought on by the texture of the structure.

The slider can be used to adjust the structure regardless of whether you are rendering the changes locally or on the entire image. This is another great new feature that makes Viveza 2 a topnotch photo editing plug-in for amateur and professional photographers to use.

## Levels and Curves

While Levels and Curves could be adjusted in the previous version of Viveza as well, this time Nik has added them directly to the interface. You can continue using Control Points while adjusting the Levels and Curves. Previously, you had to remove the Control Points before adjusting this property. Now, you can change the Levels and Curves of the areas you have selected on the image.

The main purpose of this property is to enable you to achieve a consistent tone throughout the image. Also, you can create a more refined contrast of colors and shades. As mentioned above, you can render these changes in a particular area of the image or apply it to the entire image.

## *Shadow Adjustment Enhancement*

Like Structure Enhancement, Shadow Enhancement allows you to enhance a particular image's property. In this case you have the option to enhance the shadows in the image. You can reduce the depth and darkness of the shadows around the subject and object in the image. The effect would be more natural even if you are brightening the shadows considerably.

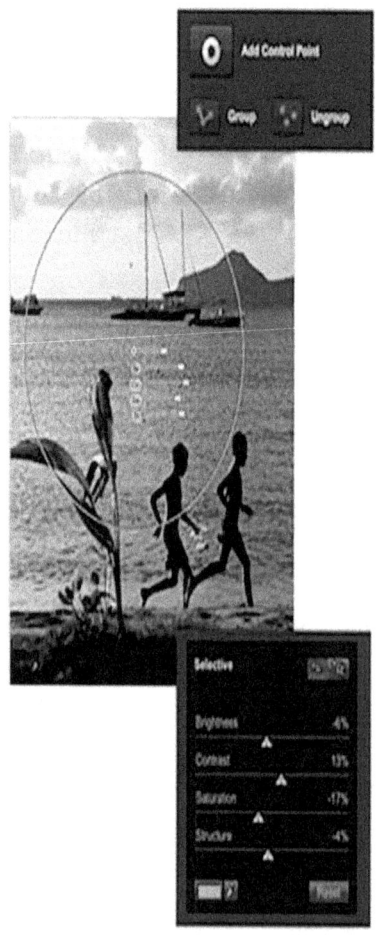

This is perhaps the most significant of all new features available to you in Viveza 2. As claimed by Nik Software, the purpose of the plug-in is to allow you to adjust the color and light in the pictures you take. There is little you can do to play with the light unless you have the ability to reduce or increase the depth of the shadows in the image.

Introduction

This is why it is crucial that you know how to work the Shadow Enhancement slider. Otherwise you won't be able to make changes to the color and light of the image. Like the other new features, this setting can also be used locally and globally.

## *Control Point Response*

Control Points are the most important feature in the Viveza plug-in and Nik has taken them up a notch in the new version. The responsiveness of the Control Points has increased considerably. This way, placing the Control Points has become much easier for you. You can select specific areas of the image on which you want to make changes.

You have the option of applying multiple Control Points on the same image and copy the changes you have made from a specific Control Point to another one. One of the chapters in the book is dedicated to Control Points and how you can use them so you shouldn't have much trouble learning to operate them.

## *Improved Interface*

Nik Software has also improved the interface of its plug-in considerably. One of the changes to the interface is the inclusion of Levels and Curves. Moreover, the Controls Panel has also been improved to make it more responsive and comprehensive to changes you make to the image, locally or globally.

The interface is clean and easy to understand. You can easily apply the changes you want to make. The major image properties can be adjusted through the sliders that you see in the interface. Overall, the interface is much better and easier to use. A chapter in the book will cover the new interface and the different options available to you through it.

How to Use Viveza 2

## *Undo & Redo*

One of the shortcomings of the original Viveza plug-in was that it didn't allow users to undo or redo the changes they had made to an image. This is a feature commonly available in all photo editing programs. Nik Software has eliminated the shortcoming by adding the Undo & Redo buttons in the interface. Now you can easily restore or remove changes to the image you are not pleased with.

This is a great feature if you make a change accidentally and have to remove it. Also, you can recover any changes you delete by mistake as well. This is one of the most significant additions to the plug-in you will find that greatly improves the user experience.

## *Selection Engine*

Nik has also improved the Selection Engine to make placing Control Points easier for you. There is little or no risk of any halos or circles emerging around the areas of the image you have selected through the Control Points. You can seamlessly add Control Points and select the areas on which you want to perform editing or make changes.

This way, you get better accuracy. This also reduces the risk of any noises emerging in the image because you failed to select the areas perfectly. In other words, you select the areas in a better way and can also make the changes you want.

These are the new features you will find in the Viveza 2 plug-in. As you can see, it is a major step up from the previous version of this plug-in. This doesn't mean that the original Viveza is not a high quality photo editing program. The changes have been

Introduction

made as Nik Software realized there was substantial room for improvement.

## Viveza 2 vs. Other Photo Editing Plug-ins

You might be wondering how Viveza 2 stacks up against other photo editing plug-ins you can find on the market. As you have seen, Viveza 2 compares quite favorably against the previous version of the plug-in. The new features and upgrades that have been made to the plug-in make it a topnotch photo editing program.

Also, Nik has made the plug-in compatible with more software than before, as you will find out in the next chapter of this book. So, how does Viveza 2 differ from other photo editing plug-ins?

The main difference between Viveza 2 and other plug-ins is that it offers selective adjustment of the different image properties as well as the color and light of the images you have taken. You can place Control Points on the image and enhance image properties the way you want to.

Moreover, the process for selecting the image and specific areas on it is also quite simple. You can even place Control Points using keyboard shortcuts that are provided later on in the book. There are no complicated selections you have to deal with. You don't have to adjust layer masks to check the changes you have made and whether they have been rendered perfectly.

When considering the plug-ins available for you to download, Color Efex Pro 4 is the closest in terms of features and settings available to you. However, where Viveza 2 holds an edge is that you can render the changes locally or globally. On the other hand, you have to ensure that the light and color settings are perfect before you can apply filters on the images you have to edit when using Color Efex Pro 4.

As you can see, Viveza 2 is superior to all other plug-ins in terms of features and controls. If you constantly feel the need to make changes to specific parts of the images you snap, this is the best plug-in you can use.

## What is U Point Technology?

U Point Technology is what allows you to use Control Points in Viveza 2 and make the necessary adjustments to the pictures you have taken. In other words, U Point Technology is the foundation for the plug-in and all the features and settings available to you. Without this technology, Viveza 2 will lose its edge in terms of selectively editing and adjusting the settings of images.

So, what is U Point Technology? The technology is basically a revolutionary method for editing and processing the images you take. It has been patented to make it exclusive to certain plug-ins. Viveza 2 is one of the leading plug-ins through which you have access to U Point Technology.

The main purpose of the U Point Technology is to make selecting different parts of the image easier. Also, you can render the changes you want quickly and without any hassle. This speeds up the process of adjusting image properties in the pictures you want to edit using the plug-in. Plus, the range of settings and image properties you can modify is greater as compared to other RGB selection tools.

Introduction

You don't have to make a complex selection every time an adjustment has to be made. Instead, you can mask it off. There are a number of changes that you can make to images, including adjusting the shadows, color balance and levels & curves. We will go over each of the changes you can make using the Viveza 2 plug-in in more detail in the coming chapters.

The U Point Technology makes the plug-in intelligent in terms of ensuring that the different image properties are cohesive and in perfect balance with each other. You can achieve the right balance between the color and light in the image using the settings available to you.

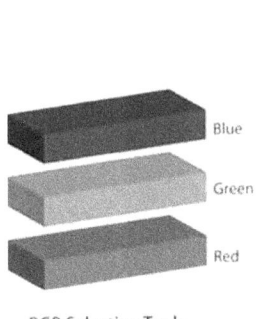
RGB Selection Tools

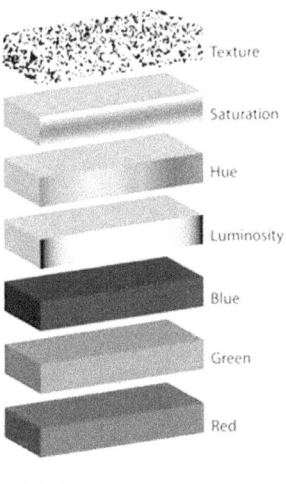
U Point™ Technology

U Point Technology in Viveza 2Viveza 2 is by no means the only plug-in in which U Point Technology has been used. However, it is one of the best you will find. As highlighted in the chapter on Viveza 2 vs. other plug-ins, there are a number of reasons why

## How to Use Viveza 2

Viveza 2 is the ideal plug-in for you to use. You can easily adjust the light and color balance in your images by changing different image properties.

The different between using U Point technology in Viveza 2 and other plug-ins is that you can selectively make changes to the image. At the same time, you can make global changes to the entire image should the need arise. This versatility is what puts Viveza 2 ahead of the pack even though the technology and features are similar to what other plug-ins have to offer.

Now that you know what Viveza is, it is time we start going over the various features it has and how you can use them to edit and adjust the properties of your images. In the next chapter, we will go over the steps you have to follow to get started with Viveza.

# GETTING STARTED

This chapter will cover the basics of Viveza. From installing the program to understanding the interface, you will find the information you need to get started with using the software.

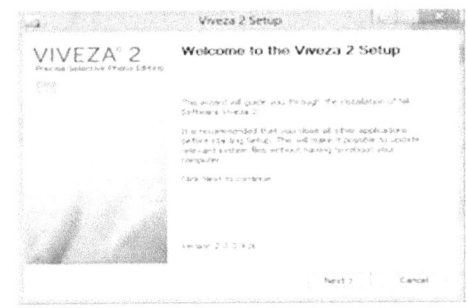

## How to Install

Viveza is compatible with leading operating systems. Regardless of whether you use Mac, Windows or Linux, you can install the software and use it without compromising on quality or performance. Moreover, all the features are available to you regardless of the operating system you are using.

Before starting the installation process, you have to install a photo editing software on your device. Viveza will then be installed as a plug-in to be used in conjunction with that particular software. The software Viveza 2.0 can be installed as a plug-in for includes:

## How to Use Viveza 2

**For Mac**

- Adobe Photoshop CS3 to CS6
- Adobe Photoshop Lightroom 2.3 to 4
- Adobe Photoshop Elements 8 to 11
- Apple Aperture 2.1 to 3.1

**For Windows**

The same software that can be used on a Mac to install Viveza is also available for Windows. The only exception is Apple's Aperture program. Moreover, Windows' users can use Adobe Photoshop CS2 as well.

You need to have any of these programs on your device before you can install and use Viveza 2.0 as a plug-in. Let's look at how you can install the plug-in.

### *Installation on Mac*

Listed below are the steps for installing Viveza 2.0 on Mac devices:

- Close any host application that you had been using. Installation requires that the only program you run is the setup.
- Open the 'dmg' file
- When the Viveza icon appears on your screen, click on it twice
- From there on, the installation wizard will guide you through the process. This makes installation easy for you so there is no reason why you shouldn't use the installation wizard.

Getting Started

- Once the process is complete, you will see a list of applications. These are the host applications that the software is compatible with.
- You will see an 'Install' icon on the screen. Click on it.
- When the installation is complete, click on 'Close'.
- Next, go to the applications tab on your screen. There you will find a new entry, Nik Software. Under Nik Software you will find the link to Viveza 2.0, indicating that the software has been installed correctly.
- To start the program, you only need to click on it once. The program will start up promptly and you can start using it.

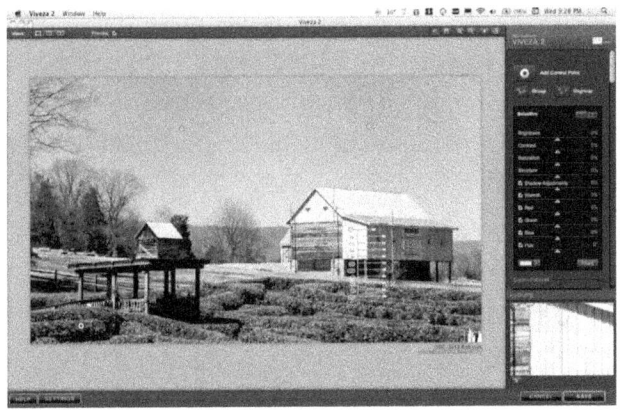

These are the steps you need to follow to install Viveza 2.0 on a Mac device. You have to make sure that you complete each and every step. Even a slight misstep could lead to improper installation. You won't be able to use it the way it is intended to be used. Moreover, some of the features might also be unavailable.

How to Use Viveza 2

## *Installation on Windows*

Here is the step by step process you have to follow for installing Viveza 2.0 on a Windows device.

- Close any host applications you might have been using at the time. The installation wizard cannot be used unless it is the only application running
- In 'Run', open the file Viveza2-pl-ver2.009all.exe
- When the file is open, it will prompt you to select a language. Choose the one you are most familiar and comfortable with to proceed
- Go for the default configuration. This will power up the installation wizard which will then guide you through the installation process. It will make things easier for you if you use the wizard rather than perform all the steps on your own. As on the Mac device, a list of host applications compatible with the software will be displayed on screen.
- Next, you will see the 'Install' button appear on screen which you have to click on
- Once the installation is complete, click on the 'Close' button
- Fire up the Start menu and look for the 'Nik Software' clicking on which will reveal the link to Viveza 2.0. Or, you can type C:\Program Files\Nik Software\Viveza 2 in the browser and it will take you to the software. Either way, the destination remains the same.
- Click on the Viveza 2 icon to start the program up. Select a free trial from the choices available and you're good to go.

Getting Started

Once the installation process is complete, you can select a free trial. The free trial is also available for Mac users when they have installed the software properly. This way, you can use the software for a certain period, usually 15 days or 1 month. You can learn to use the software in that time and then decide whether or not you want to purchase a license to use it professionally.

Since most people today use a Windows or a Mac device, learning how to install Viveza 2 on both should get the job done for you. The process has been laid out for you in detail. It is only a matter of installing the program. Following the steps described above will make installation a cakewalk for you. So, you don't have to worry about the process one bit.

## *Viveza Lightroom*

Any version of the Adobe Photoshop Lightroom from 2.3 to 4 can be used to deploy Viveza 2.0 as a plug-in. The process for this is also quite simple. Before you can start using Viveza 2.0, you have to align it with the version of Lightroom you currently have on your device. For this, you need to fire up Lightroom first of all.

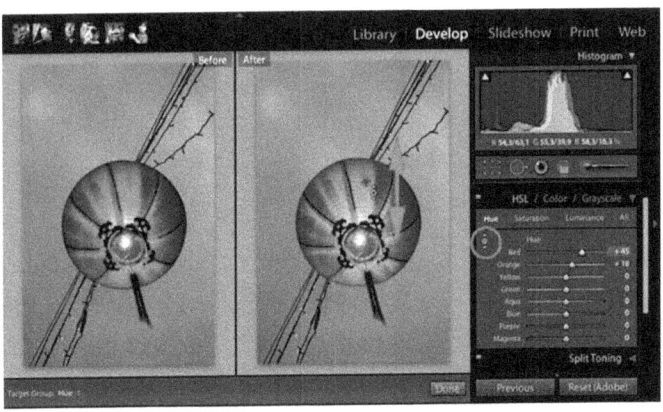

Once the program is running, go to the 'External Editor Preferences'. This is the feature that enables you to use plug-ins and other photo editing programs with the Lightroom. To find the External Editor tab, you have to first click on the 'Preferences' tab. Then, click on 'External Editing' after which you a dropdown box will appear.

Lightroom will detect any photo editing software and programs that you have installed on your device and they will appear as a list in the dropdown box. That is where you have to select Viveza 2.0. This will enable you to use the software as a plug-in in Lightroom.

There are several values that you have to input once you have selected Viveza 2.0. These are settings that apply to the photos you edit later on using the software. They include:

- Resolution
- Color Space
- File Format
- Bit Depth

There are numerous options for each of these settings. You have to set them according to your preferences. The program will provide you guidelines about the different settings you select, enabling you to make the best possible choices. Once you have set the values for each of the four settings, select the 'Update Viveza 2' option in the dropdown menu.

This is the final step and now you can close the Preferences tab. Having completed all the steps up till now, you will be able to use Viveza 2 as a plug-in for Lightroom. However, you would still have to learn how to operate the controls to adjust the colors and lighting for pictures.

## Getting Started

The first thing you have to do is to find the Library or Develop Module. Under this you will find the option to edit pictures using Viveza through Lightroom. Now, you have to find the 'Photo' tab and click on it. There are numerous options under it. You have to hover on 'Edit In'. A menu will appear to the right of the option which is where you have to select Viveza 2.

The other option you have is of right-clicking on the image you want to edit and selecting 'Edit In' or 'Open With'. Then you have to click on Viveza 2. The image will open up in the plug-in, ready to edit.

Next, you have to find the 'Edit Window'. There you will see three options under 'What to Edit'. You have to select the one at the top, namely 'Edit a Copy with Lightroom Adjustments'. You can also select one of the other two, 'Edit a Copy' and 'Edit Original' based on your needs and preferences. After selecting the option, you have to assign values for the image.

However, this is optional. You will see a 'Copy File Options' heading with the four settings, as mentioned above, listed there. They will have the settings you defined when setting up the program for future use. If you feel the need to change the values you have already assigned, you can. Otherwise, just proceed to the next step.

Once you are satisfied with the values, click on 'Edit' at the bottom of the window. Clicking on 'Edit' will fire up Viveza 2 and the image you have selected for editing will appear in front of you. You will have to save the image once again. Doing so will save a copy of the image in Lightroom, allowing you to make changes on it without tampering the original.

## Using Viveza with Photoshop

You can also use Viveza 2 as a plug-in with the main Photoshop interface. The steps you have to follow for this are somewhat different from the ones you followed for using Viveza 2 with Lightroom. The first thing you have to do is select a 'Layer'. This time, you don't have to create a copy of the layer or duplicate it. When you have finished editing the picture, Viveza 2 will automatically create a copy of it.

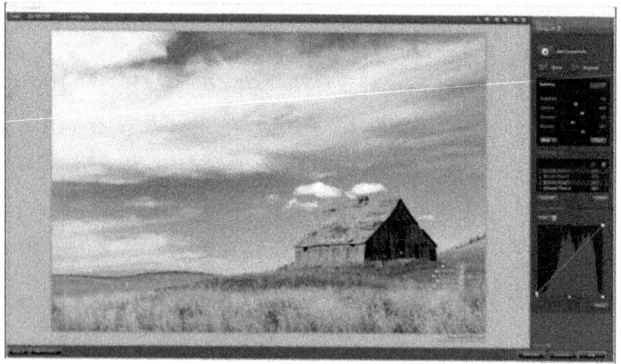

The next step is to fire up Viveza 2 in Photoshop. For this, you have to click on the Menu Filter. Under the Menu Filter, you will find a tab titled 'Nik Software'. When you click on it, 'Viveza 2' will appear. Click on it and the plug-in will launch.

You will find the image you have selected for editing open in Viveza 2, ready to edit. As with Lightroom, clicking on 'Save' will make a copy of the Layer in Photoshop. You can make any changes you want to the picture without altering the original copy.

Getting Started

## *Using Viveza with Aperture*

While Windows users have to make do with Adobe Photoshop to use Viveza 2 as a plug-in, Mac users have an additional option up their sleeve: Apple Aperture. Obviously, the process for this is markedly different than using Lightroom or Photoshop.

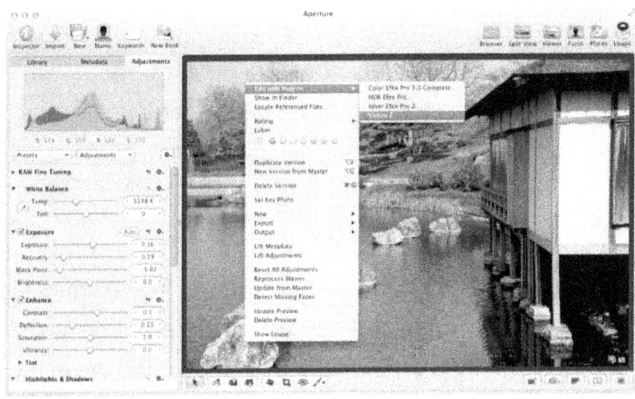

To use Aperture, you have to select the image you want to edit first. Then, you can take either of the two steps described here:

- Click on the 'Photos' menu at the top.
- Right-click on the image you want to edit.

In either case, you have to select the 'Edit with Plug-in' option. When you click on 'Edit with Plug-in', a submenu will appear. There you will find all the photo editing programs, software and plug-ins on your Mac device, including Viveza 2. Click on Viveza 2 and the image you want to edit will launch in the plug-in.

As is the case with Photoshop and Lightroom, clicking on 'Save' will launch a new copy of the picture you have selected in Aperture. You can make the changes you want to the image and then save the copy.

So, these are the steps that you need to follow to start editing images in Photoshop, Lightroom and Aperture. Although there is other photo editing software through which you can use Viveza 2 as a plug-in, these are the most popular choices. You only have to follow the steps as described above, and the images you want to edit will launch in Viveza 2.

## Viveza Interface

In order to operate Viveza 2, you have to familiarize yourself with its interface. Some changes have been made to the Viveza 2.0 interface from the first one. This is why even photographers who have used Viveza in the past should go over the new interface and the different categories to get a better idea of how things work.

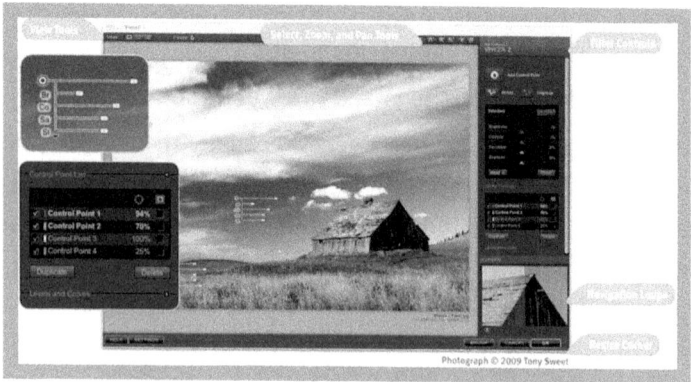

Getting Started

When you fire up Viveza 2, it will become clear to you that there are five major areas in the interface. You have to master the use of each and every one of them to be able to operate the plug-in properly. Let's look at them one by one.

## *View Modes*

The View Modes are visible on the top-left corner of the interface. As the name clearly shows, the View Modes enable you to change the way you view images you have edited. There is a 'Preview' option in the View Modes tab. Selecting 'Preview' allows you to see the edited image while deselecting it will take you back to the original image you have made changes to.

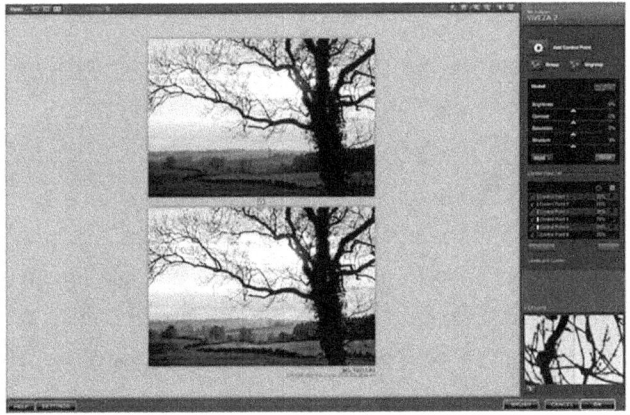

Moreover, there are three viewing options you can choose from. The main purpose of the viewing options is to enable users to compare edited images with the originals to see whether or not they need to make further changes.

- The first viewing option is the default one. In this, you get to view the entire image in the Image Area. You can choose whether you want to see the edited image or the original one by using the 'Preview' option as described above.
- The second viewing option is to see the two images in a split view. This way, you will be able to view both images at once. You can check whether the changes you made have been rendered perfectly or not.
- The third and last viewing option is side by side. As is clear from the name, this view mode enables you to view the edited and original image side to side. This gives you a better chance of comparing the two images than split or preview.

Identifying and using the View Modes is among the easiest things you have to learn when starting to use Viveza 2.

## *Image Area*

The Image Area is the spot on the screen where the image will be displayed. Now, you can choose to view a single image in the entire Image Area or opt for a split/ side by side view. You can toggle the image in the Image Area using the View Modes.

The main purpose of the Image Area is to enable you to view the changes you are making to the image in real-time. As soon as you redefine a value or alter a Control Point, the change is rendered instantly and you can see it in the Image Area. This is what gives you complete control over the editing process. You can make the changes you want without any estimation or guesswork.

*Getting Started*

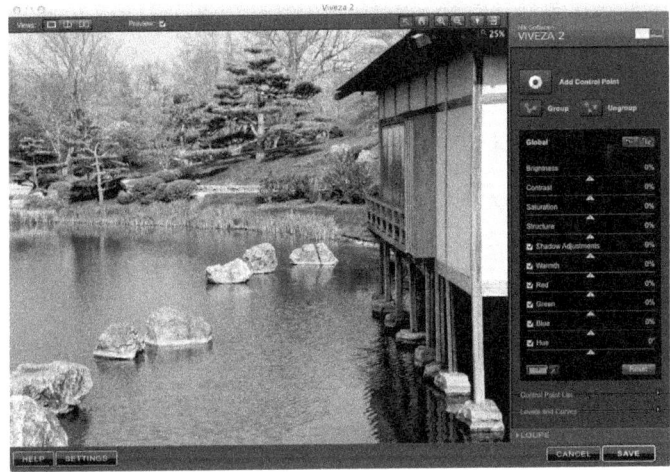

More importantly, the Image Area is the place where you can place the Control Points on the images you are editing. We will go over Control Points in greater detail in the next chapter. To give you an idea of Control Points, they are tools that enable you to change certain aspects of an image. In other words, you cannot edit an image in Viveza 2 without using Control Points.

## *Loupe & Navigation*

You won't find it hard to spot the Loupe/ Navigation panel in the Viveza 2 interface. It is at the bottom of the screen on the right side. In fact, you will see 'Loupe' written on the top with an arrow next to it. Clicking on the arrow enables you to choose between Loupe and Navigation. Another thing you will notice is that the image you are working on is displayed in this box on the right.

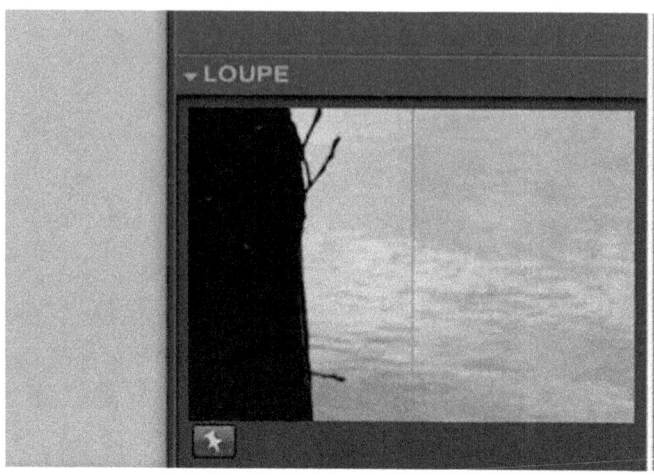

This is because this feature is also to enable you to view the image you have edited and compare it with the original picture. When you are using the Full-View mode, i.e. the Image Area is showing one picture, Loupe shows the edited image on the right with its original version on the left. When in full-view mode, the image in Loupe is displayed at 100% magnification.

When you have zoomed in on an image, this is where Navigation comes into play. Instead of viewing the entire image in the Image Area, you can view a certain part or section of it. After all, not all editing jobs will require you to make changes to entire photographs. You can use Navigation to find your way around the image and select the section you want to view in the Image Area. The image will be magnified and you will be able to see it clearly.

As is clear from the View Modes and the Loupe/ Navigation feature, Viveza 2 provides you the necessary tools to check the edited image against the original at the time of editing. You don't have to estimate whether or not you did the job right. You can

Getting Started

see the two images at the same time and observe whether or not you have to make further changes to it. This will increase the accuracy of your editing jobs as well as enable you to save time and effort.

## *Controls Panel*

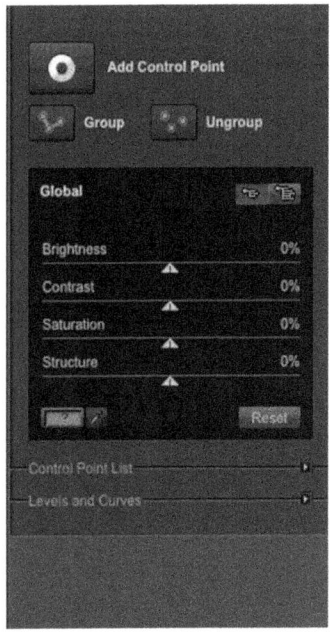

The standout feature of Viveza 2 is the Controls Panel. This is where you get to select the image area that you wish to change. You can even set the Control Points over the entire image if you want to completely revamp it. Without a doubt, the Controls Panel is the most important part of the Viveza 2 interface and you have to master it in order to make the most of this photo editing software.

The Controls Panel is in the right sidebar of the interface and quite easy to spot. You will see a number of image settings in the Controls Panel with the option to add more settings should the need arise.

As mentioned above, you can place Control Points on the image using the Controls Panel. You can do it selectively or globally, depending on your needs. You can then choose to 'Group' or 'Ungroup' the Control Points. Grouping Control Points enables you to make changes to the specific part of the image on which you have placed the points. There are further options that give you greater control over Control Points and the way you use them.

In addition to the Control Points, the Controls Panel also features Levels and Curves. You can tweak the brightness, shadow and contrast of the image as well as adjust the mid-tone. This is the main component of the plug-in and the one that determines how your pictures turn out. You are well-advised to start using it right away so you can get the hang of it.

## *Tools*

The Tools are visible right next to the Viveza 2 logo on the top right of the interface. The Tools are more to do with how you use the plug-in rather than the editing process. Yet, at the same time, it can be said that you cannot start the process without Tools. It is through these Tools that you select the image you want to edit. Moreover, it also allows you to change the position of the selected image.

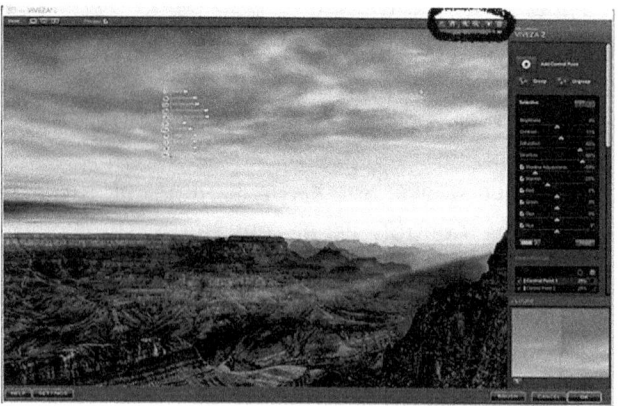

You can also adjust the view size of the image you have selected in the Image Area by zooming in or out. The icons on the Tools bar in the interface clearly display the Zoom In and Zoom Out options. You can also change the background color should you feel like it. It is not going to have any impact on the image quality.

You can also choose to hide the Controls Panel if you are not using it. An icon for this is available in Tools. This increases the width of the Image Area and gives you a better and more in-depth viewing experience. Hiding the right panel will also hide the Loupe/ Navigation feature.

These are the five main components or features that you will find on the Viveza 2 interface. You have to familiarize yourself with each of these so you can use the plug-in in the best possible way and edit your images without any hassle.

## Viveza Control

You have more or less understood how the controls in the Viveza 2 plug-in work. The one part of the controls that is yet to be covered is the global controls. One of the major changes Nik has made to the plug-in from the previous version is introducing Global controls. This means that certain controls are used for rendering changes to entire images instead of certain parts of them.

In order to make Global Adjustments, you have to use the Global controls. The next chapter covers Global Adjustments in more detail and will help you understand how things work. Coming back to the point, you have to be familiar with the controls necessary to make the Global Adjustments.

## How to Use Viveza 2

By now, you are quite familiar with how the plug-in works. We have covered the process from getting started to selecting the image you want to edit using the plug-in. From this chapter onwards, we will be looking at how you can make the adjustments and changes that you are allowed to using the Viveza 2 plug-in.

In the coming chapters, we will go through the different types of adjustments that are available to you as well as how you can use Control Points for selecting certain areas of an image. All of this information is necessary to help you understand how the plug-in works and how you can achieve the results you are looking for.

The basic premise of the Global controls is that they allow you to make changes to the entire image. This cannot be described in a simpler manner. The sliders and other adjustment tools you find in the sidebar when operating Global controls will make changes to the entire image when you increase or decrease them.

For instance, if you increase the brightness on the slider, the whole image will become brighter. Since you are making Global Adjustments, the entire image will be on display in the Image Area making it easier for you to see the changes that are being made to the picture. This way, you can see whether the changes you intended to make are being rendered properly.

Global controls differ from the local controls you have read about in the earlier parts of this chapter in the sense that the local changes only apply to certain parts of the images you select using the Control Points. Once you have mastered placing Control Points on your images, you can easily make the local adjustments you want.

The Global controls are easy to operate even if they are new for you. There is nothing different about the controls from the way they have been described above. The only thing you have to keep in mind is that they will change the entire image you have selected.

In other words, using Global controls is pretty much the same as using local controls. You only need to be aware of whether the changes are being made to the entire image or to certain parts of the image and you are good to go.

Even though the Global controls are something new for Viveza users, they are similar to what you will find in most other photo editing plug-ins. If you have used any other plug-ins apart from the ones developed by Nik Software, you will find it easier to use the controls. Even without having prior knowledge of how to use Global controls, it shouldn't take you too long to get a hang of them and use them to perfection.

Among the major Global controls you can use on Viveza 2 are:

## *Levels & Curves*

As you will recall from the first chapter of the book, Levels & Curves is another new feature you will find on the Viveza 2 plug-in. It has been introduced simply because of the Global Adjustments feature and the fact that Nik has developed Global controls to adjust the Levels & Curves in your images.

Levels & Curves appears in the right sidebar along with all the other sliders for image properties you can adjust. However, Levels & Curves is not defined as a percentage. Rather, you will have to adjust it carefully, using your observation and judgment.

The Levels & Curves adjustment is depicted exactly below the Control Point List in the sidebar. This makes it quite easy for you to spot it. When you adjust the Levels & Curves, the changes will be rendered to the whole image. You will find a dropdown box directly below the setting that enables you to select one of several image properties.

Select the one you want to change and then tweak the Levels & Curves to make the necessary changes. This is one of the major Global controls available to you through Viveza 2. As you might recall, you have the options to adjust levels and curves in Photoshop and Lightroom as well. However, Nik has made your job easier by letting you make the adjustments you want directly through the plug-in.

## *Structure*

Structure is also one of the new adjustments introduced in Viveza 2. Like Levels and Curves, Structure is also an important image property. The reason for this is that often some part of the image you have snapped doesn't turn out properly. Perhaps it is a building in the background or the clouds on the sky. In either case, you can adjust the 'Structure' and make the objects appear perfect.

When it comes to using Structure as a Global Control, it can help you smooth over any details you feel are too loud when you snapped the original picture. For instance, if you have snapped a landscape of a lawn and feel that the grass appears uneven and shadows appear in places, you can use 'Structure' to smooth it out completely. The grass will appear symmetrical and the same throughout the image.

Getting Started

Some other photo editing software on the market also allows you to adjust the structure of your images. If you have used any of them before, you shouldn't have much trouble using it in Viveza 2.

## *Hue*

Another control you can use globally is the Hue of the image. You can adjust the Hue to shift it from one angle to another. When you move the slider, the Hue of the entire image will shift. This will lead to an overall change in color for the entire image. You can adjust the Hue along the spectrum quite easily using the Global control.

As you would know, Hue is one of the most important image properties. You have to be able to adjust it both locally and globally in order to get the best results. With Viveza 2, you have the option to do so. You can change the Hue of the entire image according to your needs or selectively change the Hue of a certain part of the image.

These are some of the major Global controls available to you through the Viveza 2 plug-in. You can use them to change the properties of the images you snap without having to selectively apply the adjustments. This gives you a great deal of convenience when you have to change image properties for the entire picture rather than some parts of it.

By no means are these the only global controls you can use through Viveza 2. You will pick up on more of them as you keep using the plug-in. The plug-in is quite easy to use therefore it isn't much of a hassle for you to learn how the different controls work. So, there is no cause for concern as far as picking up the controls is concerned.

## How to Use Viveza 2

Overall, learning to use Viveza 2 involves a combination of mastering the local and global controls. We have covered both of them in some detail but there is much more to learn about both. That is what you will get in the coming chapters. As promised, the next chapters of this book are going to teach you how to make the changes and adjustments you want to your images.

We will start off with the Global Adjustments in the next chapter given that the Global controls have just been covered. This will make it easier for you to understand how the Global Adjustments are made.

# VIVEZA GLOBAL ADJUSTMENTS

Viveza has updated the control features available to its users. At the beginning of the book, we stated that the main purpose of Viveza 2 is to allow photographers to make local adjustments to their pictures. This means that they can select certain areas of the images and then make changes to it. This was the main attraction for the original Viveza plug-in as well.

## Local Adjustments

There are few, if any photo editing plug-ins available on the market that allow you to make selective changes to the images you take. Even if they do, none of them offers the level of control you get when using Viveza 2. This is why it has become the go-to program for photographers who want to touch up certain parts of their pictures.

The local controls for Viveza 2 are based on the Control Points. If you have used the original Viveza plug-in, operating the Control Points shouldn't be a problem for you at all. Many of the controls and techniques are the same as they were in the previous version of the plug-in. Even if you aren't familiar with Control Points, you will get to learn about them in the next chapter.

Just to give you a hint of the importance of Control Points, you can simply say that without knowing how to use them, you cannot use Viveza 2 effectively. That is how important Control Points are. They will allow you to make any number of local adjustments you want to your pictures. However, Viveza control for version 2.0 isn't limited to local adjustments.

## How Global Adjustments Work

This time around, Nik has introduced Global Adjustments as well. As the name suggests, you can make adjustments to the entire picture without selecting parts of it. Of course, you may need to select certain parts if they require any changes to be made. But, if you want to make some adjustments to the entire image, that can be done using Viveza 2 as well.

Previously, the process for this was a little complicated. You had to place Control Points over the entire image and then adjust the image properties you wanted to change. This rendered the changes accurately but made the process a tad bit tedious. After all, the Control Points are to be used for making local adjustments and not changes to the entire picture.

## What You Can Adjust

As listed in the first chapter of the book, Global Adjustment is one of several new features introduced in Viveza 2. This is why you need to familiarize yourself with it so that you can make optimum use of it. All the features and adjustments that you can use when

## Viveza Global Adjustments

making selective changes are available to you through Global Adjustments as well.

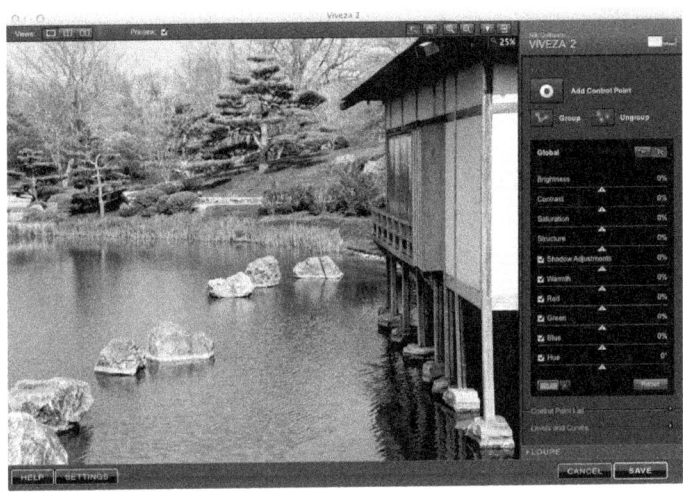

Therefore, you have the option to make the image brighter or darker, increase the hue, saturation, and color level, simply speaking adjust any of the image properties you find when hovering over the image in the Image Area. Like the other new features, this one will come in handy when the image you snap doesn't turn out the way you wanted it to.

One of the best things about Global Adjustments is that they don't cancel out the changes you make through Control Points. The opposite of this is also true. When you have made a global adjustment to an image, the change will remain intact even if you place a Control Point on the picture later on.

For instance, you snap a picture of the view outside your home. You feel that the picture is too bright, perhaps because of the sun. So, you decide to make the image a little darker to cancel out the impact the sunlight is making on it. After making the adjustment, you realize that one of the objects is hidden by a shadow.

To rectify that, you have to place a Control Point around the object and adjust the shadow level. When you are placing the Control Points to select the area, the original Global Adjustment you made, i.e. reducing the brightness of the image will remain intact. Even if the local adjustment you are making is unrelated to the global adjustment, it wouldn't be removed after placing the Control Points. This is what makes the Global Adjustment feature so effective and useful.

## How to Use Global Adjustments

In my opinion, you can make the best use of Global Adjustments by making them before moving on to local adjustments. A common mistake photographers tend to make is that they do the smaller adjustments before they correct the overall image. They place the Control Points and adjust the image properties the way they want to.

Only after that do they move towards improving the overall image. What this does is make life difficult for you. You have to be extra careful to ensure that the smaller change you made doesn't cancel out the overall adjustment you are making.

So, what we would recommend is that you make changes to the overall image and then observe whether any smaller changes are required. Taking the example of the image already mentioned that is the one you took of the view outside your home, instead of removing the shadow first and then reducing the brightness, you should go the other way around.

## Viveza Global Adjustments

In some instances, you might realize that adjusting the overall image has more or less rectified the smaller issue which you wanted to address using the Control Points. However, there will be times when moving from smaller to bigger adjustments is the best course of action for you. At the end of the day, it is up to you to decide how you want to go about doing this.

As you can see, Global Adjustments is one of the groundbreaking new features you will find in Viveza 2. This is the reason why the plug-in has become a favorite for both amateur and professional photographers. Your images will appear exactly the way you want them to appear without any noise or other issues.

Without a doubt, Global Adjustments is one of the highlights of Viveza 2. This was one feature that was definitely needed by photographers. While Viveza was a solid plug-in in its own right, Nik knew it lacked in this aspect and it duly introduced this feature.

Global Adjustments are something you will learn to make when you start using the plug-in. In my experience, making selective changes is much more difficult than adjusting properties for the entire image. Once you have mastered using Control Points, making Global Adjustments becomes a piece of cake. Don't worry; making local adjustments is covered in the following chapter.

In the next chapter, we will go over Viveza selections. You will learn how you can select different parts of the pictures you have taken and adjust them. This way, you will be able to master the skill of making changes to the entire image and also making selective changes, based on your need and preferences.

# VIVEZA SELECTIONS

As mentioned before, the Controls Panel enables you to add Control Points on the images you want to edit using Viveza 2. In this chapter, we will go over how to use Control Points. This is a crucial step in the overall user experience of Viveza 2. Without learning how to apply Control Points, you cannot use Viveza 2 to adjust the color and light of your pictures.

In other words, your Viveza 2 usage is rendered meaningless if you cannot use Control Points properly. Specifically, Control Points are intended to help professional photographers select complex objects. There are numerous other programs on the market that enable you to select an area of the image and make changes to it. However, Viveza has taken it up a notch by enabling the selection of complex objects.

## Selecting Complex Objects

Photographers can make these complex selections based on a number of factors. It is really up to you to decide on what basis you will make a particular selection. There are three main factors you can use for it:

- The texture of the image around the area where you have placed the anchor point. In this case, the texture becomes the main factor on which you can select a complex object.
- You can also use the Red, Green & Blue (RGB) values of the image in the area where you have placed the anchor point. You can take into account the saturation, hue, color, etc, of the image under the anchor point.
- You can simply create a circle using the Control Points. For this, you will have to work out the complex object you want to select and then place the Control Points accordingly. Placing them in a pattern will enable you to separate that area from the rest of the picture.

The great thing about Control Points is that they can be used with any other Nik Software Tool. Once you know how to use the Control Points, you won't face any trouble using any other version of Viveza or any other plug-in created and developed by Nik.

## Selecting Areas with Control Points

Control Points enable you to select the specific area on which the adjustments are to be made. Therefore, the first step towards mastering Control Points is to learn to select an area. There are four different ways in which you can select the area you want to edit.

### *Photoshop Tools*

- In Photoshop, you can use different tools, such as Lasso or Pen, to mark the areas in which the editing is to be done. This feature was available in the original Viveza as well. If you have used Viveza before, this shouldn't be a problem for you. You can also use the Brush to select the area.

### *Lightroom Edge Detection*

- In Lightroom, you can use Edge Detection to select the area you want to edit. This can be done using the different tools available to you, including Lightroom Brush and Magic Wand. This works pretty much the same was as selecting an area in Photoshop. If you have mastered one, you can do the other easily.

### *Color Range*

- The third method is using a color range to define the area you want to select. You will have to figure out the color properties of the area before you can do so.

### *From Viveza Interface*

- The last method is the easiest among the four. This is where you add Control Points from the Viveza interface instead of using the software in which you are using Viveza 2 as a plug-in. This method makes use of Nik's U Point technology. You will find the Control Points under the Nik Software Tools and can add them directly.

You have to decide the method of selection based on the program you are using. As you can see, the first two methods are for Photoshop and Lightroom respectively while the fourth method is for using the Viveza interface. So, you might not have the option to select a different method if you are using particular software.

Once you have selected the area you want to edit, you can change the color, lighting and other characteristics. You don't have to make changes to the entire image just because you want to touch up one corner of the picture. This makes it highly convenient for professional photographers to make adjustments to their photographs without any major inconvenience. By changing the characteristics of the selected area, you can make local edits through the Control Points.

## Adding a Control Point

Adding Control Points is a straightforward task. The Controls Panel has made it quite easy for you to add Control Points to images. Here is a step by step guide to adding Control Points:

- Find the 'Add Control Point' icon on the Panel. This is not difficult at all. Once you locate the icon, click on it. Now you can add the point on the image.

- Next, you have to click on the part of the image where you want to place the Anchor Point. The Anchor Point is the fulcrum of the selection therefore you have to select it carefully. Moreover, the properties of complex objects depend on where you place the Anchor Point. Therefore, it is even more important that you deliberate carefully where to place the Anchor Point.

- Then, you have to work the Size slider to determine the area of selection. This is done by forming a circle in that part. The size of the circle is controlled by the Size slider. When you hover over the Control Points, a number of controls will show up on screen. The Size slider is at the very top. Adjust the slider to choose the size of the circle you want to create.

Viveza Selections

By following these steps, you can add the Control Points you want on the image you have selected. It is after the Control Points have been added that you can start making edits and adjustments. Now that you have added Control Points, it is time to learn how to use them.

## Using Control Points

After you have added the Control Points, you can make the changes you want to the image you have selected. For that, you will have to understand how the Control Points are used. It is in the Control Points that you will have to make the necessary adjustments. Here are some steps you can follow to use Control Points.

- Below the Size slider, you will find 10 more sliders. These are the various image properties as discussed in the previous chapter. They will range from Brightness to Hue. These are the controls that enable you to makes changes to the image. You have to maneuver the sliders of the properties you want to change. It isn't necessary that you change all the properties. There might be some that you want to leave intact.

- In addition to the sliders appearing when you hover around the Anchor Point, the sliders are also present in the Controls Panel. You can adjust the sliders only there and make changes to the image. The properties you adjust will be reflected in the area you have selected using the Control Points.

- You can modify the position of the Control Points by adjusting the Anchor Points. This can also be done by hovering over it. Next to the Size slider, you will find the Anchor Point icon. Moving it will enable you shift its position. This way, you don't have to start the process over again if in case you place the Anchor Point in the wrong position. You can change its position later on.

There is no limit on the number of Control Points you add to an image. You can add as many as you want and in the positions you want without any restrictions whatsoever. This gives you greater flexibility, particularly when working with complex objects. For one, you can select different areas of the image and edit them separately. Moreover, the changes you make to one area do not have any effect on other areas.

Just as you have the option to add and modify Control Points, you can also delete the ones you have placed. Sometimes you may add a Control Point by mistake and find it difficult to adjust. In that case, you can simply delete. Once again, hovering over the Control Point in question will provide you the option to delete it should you want to.

Moving on from adding and using Control Points, now it is time we go over learning to manage Control Points. After all, it is more than just adding the Control Points and then adjusting the values.

## Managing Control Points

Knowing how to manage Control Points will enable you to use them in a better way. This is important if you are using Viveza 2 for editing complex objects. Here are some tips you can use to manage Control Points:

Once you have added the Control Point/s to the image, they will appear in the left panel. From there, you can make changes and adjustments to the Control Points you have selected. You will find a Control Point list there through which you can select or deselect particular ones. There are a number of different things you will see displayed in the Control Point list, including:

## *Show/Hide Checkbox (Effects)*

The checkbox is on the left of the screen, next to the place where the Control Point number is written. Ticking the checkbox will show the effects of the Control Point on the image. If you deselect a particular Control Point, its effect will remain hidden. For instance, if you have two Control Points, you can tick one and leave the other as it is, or you can select both.

## *Control Point Numbers*

The number corresponding to each Control Point you have added on the image will be displayed. For instance, the list will contain Control Point 1, Control Point 2, Control Point 3, so on and so forth. Clicking on a particular Control Point will display the selected area on the image.

## *Percentage of Area Covered*

To the right of each Control Point, you will find a certain percentage written. This shows the percentage of the image size that is encompassed in a particular Control Point. For instance, a small Control Point could be 5% of the image while a large Control Point could be 90% of the image. Typical control points are usually around 20% to 25%.

## *Selection Masks*

There is another Show/Hide checkbox, this time to the right of the Control Points list. This one is for deciding whether or not you want to see the selection mask. Checking a box will show the selection mask of that particular Control Point on the image. You can select all or none or any one of the selection masks as per your needs.

## *Delete & Duplicate*

At the bottom of the left panel, you will find two buttons titled 'Delete' and 'Duplicate'. Clicking on delete will prompt you to select the Control Point/s you want to remove from the image. As mentioned in the previous part, you can also do this by hovering over the Control Point you want to delete. You can simply press the 'Delete' key to delete a Control Point.

The 'Duplicate' button is for duplicating a Control Point. If you want to use the same Control Point in some other part of the image, you can click on Duplicate and then select the Control Point you want to duplicate. For duplication, Windows users can use the 'Control' key while Mac users will have to press the 'Option' key.

Using the left panel on the interface makes it easy for you to manage the Control Points you have added to the image. There are alternate ways for each command which you will pick up once you start using the plug-in.

So, these are the ways in which you can add, use and manage Control Points. However, there is still more to learn as we have yet to go over the methods for grouping Control Points.

Viveza Selections

# Grouping a Control Point

As described above, control points enable you to select the parts of the picture that you want to make changes to. However, sometimes the changes to be made are complex and hard to render using simple control points. This is where you have to be able to group control points. You can then use multiple tones and colors to adjust the image.

When you group a series of control points, a set of sliders appear on the screen. The adjustments apply to each area you have selected. Moreover, there is a 'Size' slider. The 'Size' slider is the only one that can be applied to individual control points. The sliders are the same as described in the previous part. You can adjust the different properties of the image in the area you have selected.

### *Why Group Control Points?*

As you have read in the previous part of this chapter, adding and using Control Points is not difficult at all. As long as you follow the steps described above, you shouldn't have any hassle doing so. So, why then should you have to learn about grouping Control Points? Wouldn't working on one Control Point at a time be better than grouping all of them together?

There are a couple of reasons why learning to group Control Points is important.

- Firstly, you don't have to work on each individual Control Point. This will save you considerable time and effort, especially if you want to make the same changes to each Control Point. You only need to click on one of

the Control Points in the group, adjust the sliders and the change will be applied to all the Control Points.
- You can adjust the size of each Control Point separately. This gives you the flexibility of using Control Points of various sizes to suit your needs. You can use any combination of Control Points you want.
- Handling complex and large photo projects becomes easier when you can group Control Points together. As mentioned before, making the same change to different parts of an image becomes simpler when you only have to adjust one slider.

Furthermore, you have the option to ungroup the Control Points should you feel the results are not to your liking. It isn't as if you would have to use the group just because you created it. You can discard it and work on individual Control Points if that makes things easier for you.

The only drawback, if you can call it that, of grouping Control Points is that it cannot be used when you place one or two Control Points. That being said, Nik probably intended the grouping option to be used when a photographer has to work with a large number of Control Points. Keep in mind that there is no limit on the number of Control Points you add to an image. Grouping them will make it easier for you to make necessary changes and adjustments without having to spend too much time on it.

Without a doubt, grouping Control Points is a skill you should learn. It will only enhance your experience of using the Viveza 2 plug-in. Moving on to the business end of things; let's look at how you can group Control Points.

Viveza Selections

## *Creating a Group*

The technique for adding Control Points to an image will not be useful when you are creating a group. This is why you have to unlearn that in order to group Control Points. The basic idea remains the same so it is not exactly a different method. You have to carefully pick out the Control Points and click on the image in the places you want to add them.

To create a group of Control Points, you have to follow these steps:

- Using the Shift Click, add the Control Points on the image. Make sure that you are using the Shift Click throughout or multiple Control Points will not be added on the image. You can also select the Control Points on the left panel.

- Next, you have to locate the 'Group' icon which is in the Controls Panel on the right side of the interface. Clicking on 'Group' will automatically create a group of Control Points. The multiple Control Points you selected in the first step will be part of the group.

- Once the group has been created, an outline will appear around all the Control Points. The area in which all the Control Points are located becomes the 'Super Control Point' and the outline, of a faint yellowish color, illustrates this.

- The 'Super Control Point' can be adjusted and changed as per your requirements. You can control the Control Points in the group using the Super Control Point.

These are the four steps you have to follow to group Control Points. As you can see, it isn't too difficult.

## *Using the Group*

Now that you have created the group, it is time you learned how to use it. This is also made easier by the fact that you can control all the different Control Points through the Super Control Point. You don't have to deal with each Control Point individually. Here are some tips on using a Control Point Group.

- To adjust the image in the Control Points you have selected, you have to use the sliders that appear on the screen when you hover over the Super Control Point. These sliders are also present in the Controls Panel so you can use them there as well. Any adjustment you make using the sliders will apply to all the Control Points in the group.

- For instance, if you decrease the brightness on the slider, the effect will appear in all the areas you have selected on the image using Control Points. Same goes for other values you can adjust through the sliders, including RGB, Hue, Saturation, etc.

- You have to remember the fact that only the image properties can be changed by adjusting the sliders. Changes to the values will be rendered on the Control Points. However, if you want to change the size or position of a Control Point, you will have to select it individually and then adjust the Size slider.

- You can show or hide the effect of a selection mask using the Control Point list. This will be done the same way as in the previous part. The only difference is that the Control Points are in the same group and their values can be changed simultaneously.

Viveza Selections

- So, before you use the Control Point list to show or hide the selection masks, you have to find the 'Group' icon in the left panel. Only then will you be able to use the show/hide checkboxes for your group. The same process will be followed to show/hide the effects of the changes you have made to each Control Point.

Even using the Control Point groups is not difficult as you can see. Follow the tips listed here to make things easier.

## Deleting a Group or Ungrouping Control Points

There can be instances where you don't want to use the group of Control Points you have created or maybe the group didn't turn out the way you wanted it to. In that case, you can either delete the group altogether or ungroup the Control Points and start over.

For deletion, you simply have to select the group you want to delete. Pressing the 'Delete' key will do the job. One thing you do need to keep in mind is that deleting a group will also delete all the Control Points in it.

For ungrouping Control Points, you have to select the particular Control Points you don't want to be part of the group. In this case, you can select all the Control Points if you want to remove all of them. Otherwise, select the ones you want to remove from the group and then click on 'Ungroup'. The 'Ungroup' icon is present in the right sidebar and shouldn't be hard to find.

When ungrouping, you can retain some of the Control Points you selected on the image unlike in the case of deleting the group.

This is how you can create, use and delete Control Point groups. With this, we come to the end of our chapter on Control Points. As you will have observed by now, it is the most important part of learning to use Viveza 2. Therefore, you have to pay special attention when following the steps outlined for the various things you can do using Control Points.

In the next chapter, we will build on the use of Control Points and learn how you can change the color of the areas you have selected in an image.

# CHANGING THE COLOR OF THE SELECTED AREAS

The purpose of selecting an area on the image using Control Points is to enable you to change the image properties in that part of the picture. This way, you can match different parts of the picture and also create a contrast, should you feel the need to. At the same time, you can also change the color of the selected area. This is one of the standout features of Viveza 2 and can really help you change the way the image appears after you have worked on it.

The most common reason one would want to change the color of a particular area in an image is to match it with some other part. For instance, if your background is black and the color of the object/ subject does not appear the way you want it to, you can change either the color of the background or the object. This gives you even more control over the end result you produce by using the plug-in.

How to Use Viveza 2

This is why it is imperative that you master the use of Control Points. It is only through them that you can selectively change the color of a certain area in the picture. Of course, you have the option of setting a Control Point group over the entire image and changing its color altogether should you feel like doing so. Regardless of why you want to change the color of an area in the image, it is important that you do it in the best way possible.

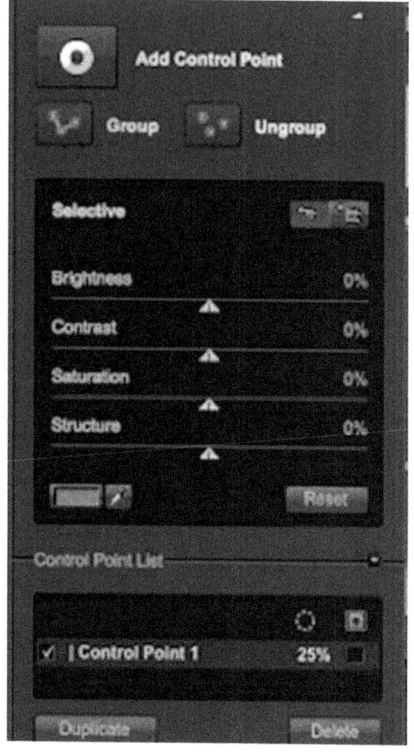

Here are a few tips you can follow to selectively change the color of an area in the picture using Control Points:

- Place the Control Points around the area of the picture you want to change the color of. Make sure that you have placed the Control Points accurately to ensure there is no overlap. Needless to say, it isn't a pleasant sight if the color of the image changes without you intending it to. Therefore, follow the steps listed before for placing Control Points to the letter. Moreover, you should group the Control Points in case that appears to be the best option to select the area properly.

Changing the Color of the Selected Areas

- Once you have placed the Control Points, the options for changing the color of that particular area will appear in the Controls Panel. This is where you will find the other adjustments you can make as mentioned in the previous part of this chapter. Now, there are two different options available to you with regards to choosing the color you want to insert into the selected area.

## *Using the Color Picker*

- There is a rectangular box in the side bar opposite the Reset button. The box has a '?' in the middle. You have to click on the box to get the list of colors that you can choose to add to the area you have selected using Control Points. The box, when you place the Control Points, will display the main color around the particular Anchor Point.
- Clicking on the box reveals the Color Picker from which you can select the color you want to add to the area. There are a variety of options available so you won't have much trouble finding the one you are looking for. Selecting the color will automatically render the changes in the area you have marked using the Control Points so you can check it right away.

## *Using the Eye Dropper*

The second option you have is to use the Eye Dropper. The Eye Dropper has a syringe-like symbol and is located right next to the Color Picker box, so it shouldn't be too hard for you to spot. The difference here is that you don't get a list of colors to choose from. Rather, you have to select a color from a different part of the image.

What this means is that instead of applying a color from the options available to you via the plug-in, you can pick any color from a different section of the picture. This option is ideal in situations where you have to match the colors of different parts of the picture perfectly.

You only have to specify the two areas, i.e. one from which you will select the color and the other to which the color would be applied. This is how you can change the color of the area you have selected using the Control Points. These are the two options available to you when it comes to changing the color of the areas you select on the image using Control Points. Like I said before, it gives you greater control over finding the perfect balance between the different colors present in the image.

No longer do you have to contend with pictures that lose their appeal simply because the colors don't match properly. With this top of the line plug-in, the changes are rendered perfectly without any of them visible to the naked eye. This is another great task that can be performed by placing Control Points on the images you open via Viveza 2.

With this we come to the end of our chapter on Control Points and their various uses. Given that you have received all the information you require about Control Points, there shouldn't be any trouble for you when using them. Only make sure that you follow the instructions carefully.

# VIVEZA ADJUSTMENTS

The great thing about Viveza 2 is that the adjustments you make are rendered in such depth and detail that one assumes they were there in the original pictures. This is one of the numerous benefits of using this plug-in. You have complete freedom to make any number and type of changes you want to make.

When it comes to adjusting your images, the key is to ensure that you master the use of each particular image property so that you can achieve the desired effect on the image. With Viveza 2, you can adjust 11 different image values individually. Each of them has a different effect on the image; therefore you need to work out how you are going to use them.

As you know, you have to select the area(s) of the picture you want to make changes to. This is done by adding Control Points to the image. Regardless of whether you are using 1 Control Point or a hundred, you have to place them before you can start tampering with the image properties. Use the information from the previous chapter to apply the Control Points properly.

## Brightness

As you may know, Brightness is the perception of how you see an object reflecting light or glowing. In an image, sometimes the main subject or object is not bright enough or is too bright. In this case, you have to adjust the brightness settings to get it to appear perfect.

Now, you have two options. You can either change the brightness of the background or of the object itself. It depends on how you feel the quality of the image can be improved. The process remains the same. You have to place a Control Point around the area where you want to adjust the brightness.

In the case of adjusting the brightness of the foreground, grouping various Control Points is a good idea as it enables you to cover a larger area. On the other hand, if you only want to change the brightness of the object, place a Control Point there. Brightness is one of the foremost sliders that appear when you hover over the image.

Let's take an example of how you can adjust the brightness to change the quality of an image. You have snapped a picture of a family outdoors on a sunny day. The sunlight might be pervading all areas of the picture. Your clients could get lost in the glare. What you can do here is reduce the brightness of the area of the picture where the family is standing.

Conversely, if it is dark around them and visibility is an issue, you can increase the brightness of the surroundings to improve light. You can also increase the brightness of the family.

Viveza Adjustments

# Contrast

Viveza 2 has been designed to help you achieve the best possible contrast between the light and color in the pictures you take. As mentioned at the outset, the main purpose of the plug-in is to provide professional photographers the tools they need to touch up their images and improve quality.

The contrast in an image is the difference between the colors of the objects and subjects in the picture and the lighting around them. Achieving the perfect balance between the two is important to get the image right. For this, you can use the contrast slider on the Viveza 2 interface.

If you feel the colors in a picture are too bold compared to the lighting, you can increase the contrast to make it more collusive. Similarly, you can reduce the contrast should you feel the lighting and colors appear too 'loud'. You can make the background duller and the foreground brighter and vice versa.

The bottom-line is that increasing the contrast of an image makes the highlights appear much brighter. At the same time, the shadows become deeper and darker, which is the reason why the highlights appear so bright.

In case there are no visible shadows in the image you are editing in Viveza 2, increasing the contrast would actually reduce the contrast. Confused? The reason for this is that there are no shadows in the picture to be contrasted with the highlights. As a result, the contrast is between the highlights. When you increase the contrast, the highlights get compressed and lose contrast.

## Saturation

In many ways, saturation is quite similar to contrast. The main difference is that it is used to 'separate' the colors in the image. When you increase the saturation of an image or an area of it, the brightness and contrast also increase. Also, the image appears much sharper. Reducing the saturation on the contrary reduces the brightness and contrast, therefore making the image duller.

When using the saturation slider in Viveza 2, you will notice that it has a prominent impact on the parts of the image where the colors are more vibrant and bold. For instance, if you have bright red in some part of the photo, place a Control Point around it and increase or decrease the saturation. The effect will be quite drastic.

In contrast, by reducing or increasing the saturation of an area where the colors are less vibrant or dull, like gray or black, the effect wouldn't be as pronounced. So, if you feel the background is too bright as compared to the object/subject, you can increase the saturation for it. This will cause the background to get duller and the object/subject to appear prominently.

## Red, Green & Blue (RGB)

The Red, Green & Blue (RGB) image property is commonly edited by photographers. Based on the three primary colors, changing the RGB levels by using the slider in Viveza 2 adjusts each of the three colors in the image.

Regardless of location, object and surroundings, each image you snap will have some element of the three primary colors. Changing the slider will enable you to understand just how they affect the color and lighting of your photo.

Viveza Adjustments

My recommendation is that you leave RGB as the last adjustment. Typically, you will find you can make the desired changes to images using other sliders, such as Brightness, Saturation and Hue. Only if you have used RGB before and are familiar with its impact on an image should you use it.

The great thing about the RGB settings in Viveza 2 is that you can adjust them all separately. You don't have to render the changes at the same time which gives you greater control. For instance, if you want to adjust the Red setting, you can do so using the slider available in the Controls Panel. Same goes for the Blue and Green setting as well.

When you adjust one of the colors, the change will appear in the image. You can see for yourself whether the change has been made the way you intended it. You can go through all three colors one after the other and decide if all of them have to be changed or if adjusting even one of the three can achieve the desired results.

## **Structure**

If you have used the Sharpener Pro from Nik Software, you will be familiar with Structure Adjustment. Nik has added this adjustment to the Viveza 2 plug-in to make it more comprehensive. This is one of the several new adjustments that you will find in the plug-in. Once again, Viveza users will have to start from scratch to learn how this adjustment works.

Basically, the purpose of the Structure Adjustment is to enhance details of the structures, including the objects and subjects in the images you take. What this means is that if a structure gets lost in the shadows or doesn't appear cohesive with the rest of the

## How to Use Viveza 2

image, you can use the Structure slider and increase or decrease the level of detailing.

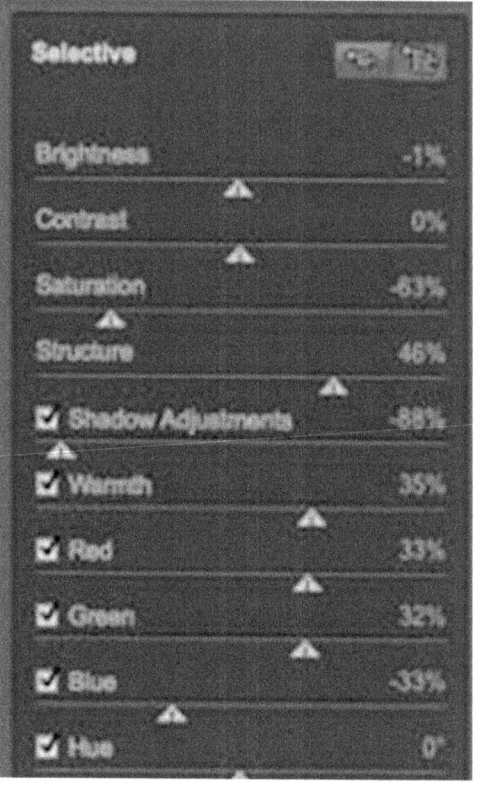

The great thing about the Structure Adjustment is that at no point does it appear that the image has been tampered with or processed to achieve the level of detailing that is visible. This is what makes this feature a great tool for professional photographers to use.

Another aspect of the Structure Adjustment you are bound to appreciate is that no artifacts are added to the image when you make the adjustment. This is the case with some other photo editing programs. A halo appears around the point where the adjustment has been made or an object shows up. In either case, the original image loses its appeal and it becomes quite evident that some touching up has been done.

Yet, this is not the case when you adjust the Structures in your images through the Viveza 2 plug-in.

Viveza Adjustments

## Shadows

If you are a perfectionist, you will find this particular adjustment very useful. Often you will notice that some details are left out when you edit an image. For instance, if you increase the depth of an object, it may appear out of place with its surroundings. This is where adjusting the shadow on the object can help you out.

The adjustments for Shadows and Highlights are available in Lightroom and Photoshop. However, to use them with Viveza 2 would mean having to edit the image twice. Nik has removed the need for this by introducing the Shadow Adjustment Slider in Viveza 2.0. Now, you can conveniently adjust the highlights and shadows that appear out of place in your images.

The most important use of the Shadow Adjustment slider is when you darken any part of the image. Some of the details of the image will get lost in adjustment. For instance, the hair of a person or the appearance of the grass might change when you adjust the brightness or depth of the image. You can rectify this using the slider.

You only need to increase or decrease the Shadow to render the changes you are looking for. As mentioned before, this will prove to be quite useful for photographers who pay special attention to detail. Now, none of the details of your image will be lost regardless of the adjustments and changes you make to it.

## Warmth

You can add warmth to your pictures using the Warmth Adjustment slider. Sometimes, the images you snap are too dreary and cold to be personable and you want to make them appear brighter and warmer. You can do that without having to adjust any of the other image properties by simply toggling the Warmth Adjustment slider.

This works the other way as well. If you want to decrease the warmth in an image, you can easily do that by moving the Warmth slider to the left. As you may know, warmer pictures allow the viewers to connect with them on an emotional and personal level. Moreover, it may suit the image you have taken to be warmer.

Let's say you have taken a picture of the sunset during fall or winter. Now, the image might appear perfect to look at but you know that the sun isn't as warm and bright as it is during the summer and spring seasons. This is where you can increase the warmth of the image and add a little more sun to the sunset.

In contrast, you can use the same adjustment to tweak the skin tone of a person lying on the beach. For instance, if you have taken the picture of a person soaking in the sun, you can actually enhance the effects of the sun on his/her skin by decreasing the warmth. Simply speaking, you can add a little tan to the skin.

The bottom-line is that you can use this adjustment to warm or cool your images.

## Hue

The Hue adjustment is one of the most important controls you get through Viveza 2. If ever your photos go horribly wrong, this is one of the adjustments that will help you restore them. When you adjust the Hue slider, you will notice that the colors in the image will change along a spectrum.

Viveza Adjustments

This is why the Hue slider has degrees next to it instead of a percentage. This is because the Hue is changed along a spectrum. You can adjust the angle you want the Hue to be changed to and the adjustment will be rendered. You can play around with different angles to determine which Hue setting works best for your images.

You will note that the black & white and grey areas in your images won't be affected by the Hue adjustment unless you are applying it globally. You will see different results for each level of Hue you adjust. My suggestion to you is to use a test image to learn all you can about the different Hue settings. This is one adjustment you shouldn't risk making on the final copy without prior experience.

Trial and error can only get you so far so you have to make sure that you know what you are doing. Along with RGB and Shadow Adjustment, it is Hue that can help you improve the quality of your images significantly. Once you know how to use the Hue slider perfectly, you can restore the color of the most bland images you have taken.

## Levels & Curves

Finally, we come to the Levels & Curves adjustment. This is one of the major additions to the Viveza 2 plug-in that will help you change the very appearance of your images. The main purpose of the Levels & Curves adjustment is to help you adjust the tone of the image. This again is an adjustment that enables you to discover the optimal color balance in the images you are editing.

Using this adjustment, you can play with the contrast of the colors. If you want to get a leg up on this adjustment, you can use the one provided in Photoshop. That will give you an idea of how the Levels & Curves Adjustment works. As you will see when working on the plug-in, a curve appears as part of a diagram when you are working on the Levels & Curves.

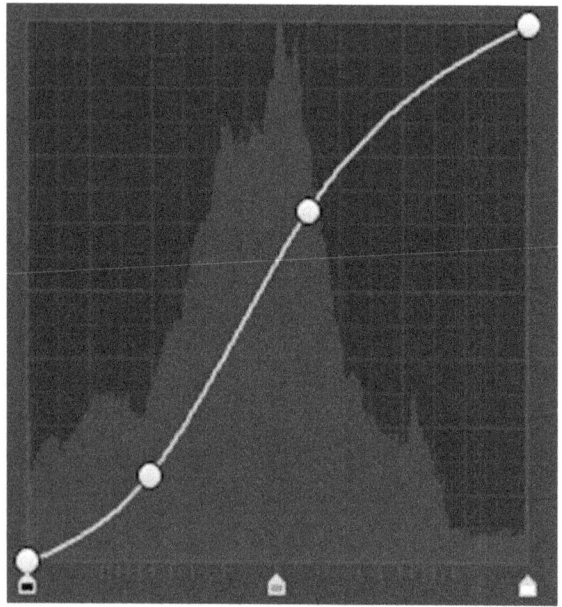

You have to tweak the curve to adjust the Levels & Curves. For instance, if you want to increase the level of contrast, you have to modify the curve till it takes on an S-Shape. The opposite will work if you want to reduce the contrast in the image. The diagram to the right shows how the curve should appear.

When working on Levels & Curves, you can select from any of the different image properties using the dropdown box. The curve you see here is for the RGB of the image.

## Viveza Adjustments

These are the nine different adjustments available to you through the Viveza 2 plug-in. As you can see, they cover the entire range of image properties you might want to change to achieve the desired results. Nik has upped the game by introducing a number of new adjustments. Now that you are familiar with all of them, it shouldn't be too difficult for you to start using them to your advantage.

At the same time, you should keep in mind that just because you can make all these adjustments doesn't mean you absolutely have to. Be selective and only make the changes that need to be made. Or else, you would waste your time and effort without achieving anything productive.

The next chapter brings to light the keyboard shortcuts that will improve your experience of using the plug-in.

# KEYBOARD SHORTCUTS

Using Viveza 2 can become much easier if you familiarize yourself with the different keyboard shortcuts available. Instead of having to use the mouse to control all the different features and settings, you can apply them directly from your keyboard. The great thing is that keyboard shortcuts are available for both Windows and Mac devices.

## Keyboard Shortcuts for Windows

The following table displays the keyboard shortcuts you can use on a Windows device. The left column depicts the action and the right column the keys you have to press to perform that action.

| | |
|---|---|
| Add Control Point | Ctrl + Shift + A |
| Delete Control Point | Backspace |
| Duplicate Control Point | Ctrl + D, Alt + drag, or Ctrl + C to copy, then Ctrl + V to paste |

How to Use Viveza 2

| Apply Filter | Enter |
| --- | --- |
| Cancel Filter | Esc |
| Full Screen | F |
| Pan Tool | H or Spacebar |
| Preview | Ctrl + P |
| Show/Hide Palettes | Control Tab |
| Select Tool | A |
| Undo | Ctrl + Z |

These are the keyboard shortcuts you can use to make the changes listed here on your Windows computer.

## Keyboard Shortcuts for Mac

Here are the keyboard shortcuts you can use on your Macintosh devices. The layout of the table is the same as that for the table for the keyboard shortcuts for Windows.

| Add Control Point | Cmd + Shift + A |
| --- | --- |
| Delete Control Point | Delete |
| Duplicate Control Point | Cmd + D, Option + drag, or Cmd + C to copy, then Cmd + V to paste |
| Apply Filter | Enter |
| Cancel Filter | Esc |

Keyboard Shortcuts

| | | |
|---|---|---|
| Full Screen | | F |
| Pan Tool | | H or Spacebar |
| Preview | | Cmd + P |
| Show/Hide Palettes | Control | Tab |
| Select Tool | | A |
| Undo | | Cmd + Z |

As you can see, there are keyboard shortcuts available for all major functions that can be performed in the Viveza 2 plug-in. They make it quite convenient for you to edit the images you want to make changes to.

When working on a series of images, going back and forth to use the mouse to make changes can prove to be a bit cumbersome. This is where using keyboard shortcuts improves the user's experience and makes it easier for you to make the changes you want.

In the next chapter, we will go over some examples of how you can use the plug-in to make changes to your images. They will make it clearer how Viveza 2 can be used to make certain adjustments.

# EXAMPLES

In this chapter, we will move on to some practical uses of the Viveza 2 plug-in. By now, we have covered most of the controls and features available to you through the plug-in. This is the best time to start depicting how the changes you make will be rendered in the images you are editing.

We will go over two examples in this chapter. One is for a local adjustment you can make and another one for a Global Adjustment. Here is an overview of some common examples of photo editing using the Viveza 2 plug-in:

## Making the Sky Darker

We have highlighted this example a couple of times before as well. This is one of the most common adjustments photographers have to make to enhance their images. Sometimes the sky is not dark enough for the subjects and objects in the picture. You can easily touch it up using the adjustments available to you through the plug-in.

The reason why learning to darken the sky is important is because it makes the image appear more dramatic. In some instances, the clouds and sky appear saturated and it seems as though they have the same color tone. Even though the picture is natural and no effects have been rendered, it does make it appear as though you have processed it.

The two images below show the effect of darkening the sky. In the first image, the sky is lighter. This is the picture the photographer took. In the second image, you will see how the changes have been rendered to make the sky appear darker and more impactful. This is after the image was processed using the Viveza 2 plug-in.

Examples

This is how darkening the sky makes your images appear more impactful than they actually are. It can make a world of a difference to the final image. So, how do you go about darkening the sky in your images? Here is a step-by-step process you can follow:

- Add a Control Point on the image at the spot where you want to darken the sky. Generally, the Control Point is placed where the sky is bluest. You have to darken the blue area to make the image appear more impactful.
- The first adjustment you have to make is to reduce the brightness. Move the slider towards the left to reduce the brightness in the part of the image you have selected with the Control Point.
- To make the reduced brightness appear in sync with the rest of the image, you will have to increase the contrast. This time, you have to move the Contrast slider to the right.
- Reducing the brightness of the sky will make it appear duller. This might cause it to lose some of its 'blueness'. To adjust this, you have to increase the Saturation of the image. The sky will become bluer as the colors saturate to the point where the tone becomes consistent with the overall image.
- Once you have adjusted the Control Point, it is time you increase its size. Use the Size slider to increase the reach of the Control Point so that it covers the entire sky. You need to render the changes to the whole sky or else there will be some inconsistencies when the final image appears. Of course, you can place a large Control

Point that covers the sky. However, rendering accurate changes is easier on a smaller area.

- You can simply copy the Control Point you have adjusted and paste it on other parts of the image where the sky appears. This is done to ensure that you can make the required adjustments with the least amount of effort. Moreover, this ensures that the tone and color of the sky appears consistent throughout the image.
- The last thing you need to do is add a Control Point to the foreground. When you are adjusting the background, it is important that you make sure that the same changes don't affect the foreground.

These are the steps you have to follow to make the sky darker in the images you edit. As you can see, it isn't too difficult a task. Make sure that you follow the steps in the right order so that you achieve the desired results. This is one of the most helpful local adjustments you can learn to make with the Viveza 2 plug-in.

For our next example, we are going to look at a global adjustment you can make.

# Improving Contrast & Color

In some cases, you have to work on the entire image to improve the light and color. One of the foremost Global Adjustments available to you through Viveza 2 is adjusting the Contrast and Color. Keep in mind that this example is for applying changes globally. It may not work out the way you want it to if you make it using Control Points. Therefore, restrict yourself to using it globally.

Examples

In the two images below, you will see how the color of the ocean water has been modified using the Contrast slider. In the first image, you see the original color of the ocean, a grayish blue. In order to make the image more appealing, the photographer increased the contrast which made the water appear bluer.

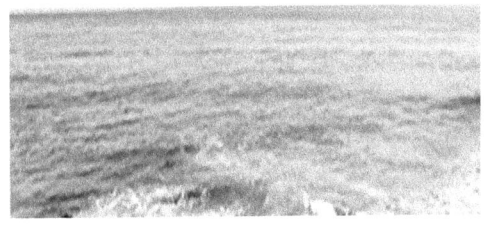

Let's say you have taken the picture of the coastline from the edge. The picture includes the skyline as well as the rolling waters along with the embankment. In such a picture, you will have the color of the sky, the ocean as well as the grass on the coast. Plus, you might also have to adjust the color of the rocks and other structures on the coastline.

With such a large number of adjustments to be made, using Global Adjustments is the way to go. Since you don't have to add any Control Points to the image, the process is much simpler. Here are the steps you have to follow:

## How to Use Viveza 2

- Increase the Contrast in the image by dragging the slider to the right. When you increase the contrast, the dark areas of the image will become darker and the lighter areas will become brighter. This is the perfect contrast setting you can use to adjust the colors in your images. The great thing is that other image properties like Saturation will not be affected.
- The next step is to increase the Saturation of the image. This is done to make the colors appear more vibrant and improve the overall tone. Since you have increased the Contrast, enhancing the Saturation is important to stay consistent with the original color tone.
- The third step is to increase the Structure of the image. This is done to improve the texture of the objects present within the image. Changing the Contrast and Saturation is bound to affect their appearance. This is why you have to level them out, which can be done by using the Structure slider.

These three adjustments allow you to adjust the Contrast and Color of your images. This is perhaps the easiest way you can make the desired changes. In case you are adjusting an image which shows the skyline, as referred to in the example provided in the beginning, it is a good idea to add a Control Point to darken the sky to make it more impactful. When you improve the Contrast and Color of the overall image, the sky may not appear the way you want it to.

These are a couple of examples that will come in handy when you start editing your images using Viveza 2. The next chapter is the last one for this book. You will find some expert tips that will enhance your user experience significantly.

# EXPERT TIPS

The purpose of this book is to familiarize you with the Viveza 2 photo editing plug-in and how you can use it. As you have read from the beginning, we have covered pretty much all there is with regards to being able to operate the controls, both local and global. Yet, there are some expert tips that will come in handy that you need to know.

## Selecting the Adjustments

This point has been highlighted to a certain extent in one of the earlier parts of the book but it is possible you may have overlooked it given the fact that there is so much to go through. As you would recall in the chapter on Viveza adjustments, there are a number of sliders you will find in the sidebar you can use to change image properties.

However, the changes aren't going to be rendered till you actually select the particular adjustment you are going to make. Even though the adjustments appear as soon as you select an image, the changes are only applied when you check the box next to the particular adjustment. If you leave the box unchecked, the changes will not appear in the Image Area.

## How to Use Viveza 2

As you can see in this image, three adjustments have been selected, namely Green, Blue and Hue. Since the boxes next to each of them are checked, it means that changes the user makes will appear on the image that has been selected. This way, you can use the slider to make necessary adjustments.

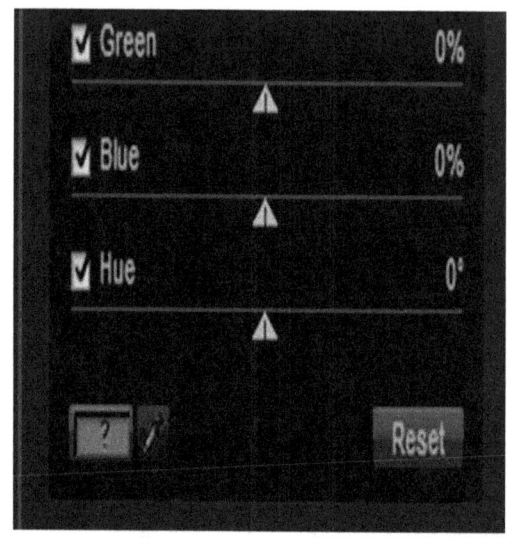

On the other hand, leaving the box unchecked would disable the adjustment altogether. In other words, this is how you can hide the sliders you don't want to use.

In this image, you can see that Shadow Adjustments has been checked which means the user can adjust the shadows in the image. On the other hand, Warmth has been unchecked. You will note that the name of the adjustment has dimmed a bit. This is what is meant by hiding a slider. You cannot adjust the Warmth of the image unless you check the box.

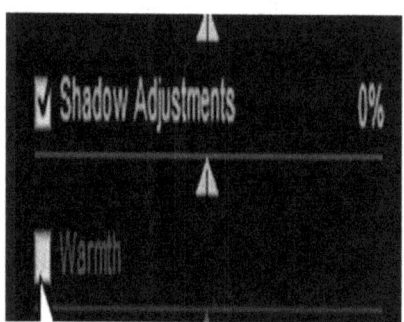

Expert Tips

## Saving Money on Buying Viveza 2

This tip is not related to using the plug-in but is one that will come in handy. You might recall that the pricing structure of the Viveza 2 plug-in has been mentioned in the first chapter of the book. The price for the plug-in is $199.95. When you take all the features and adjustments you get through Viveza 2, the price is quite reasonable by all means.

That being said, you can actually get Viveza 2 for a significantly lower price. If you already have Viveza installed, you can upgrade to the newer version for $99.95. Even if you don't have the original Viveza, you can still enjoy this significant cost saving.

The first thing you should do is buy the original Viveza plug-in. The reason for this is that it is available for around $25. Once you install it, you can upgrade to Viveza 2. There is no restriction on the length of time for which you should have been using Viveza before you can upgrade to the second-generation plug-in.

Combining the cost of buying the original plug-in and the upgrade, you can still save over $70 on buying the plug-in. This makes the deal even sweeter for you. You can get a top of the line photo editing plug-in at an affordable price.

## Follow the Installation Wizard

You might take this for granted but some users have missed out on the great features the Viveza 2 plug-in offers by not following the installation wizard. Most of them are the photographers who have used Viveza in the past. They were under the assumption that the installation process for Viveza 2.0 would be the same as that for the original plug-in.

However, this is not the case at all. Among the new features you get with the Viveza 2 plug-in is a new installation process. For the original Viveza plug-in, you had to install two copies of the plug-in. One was for using with Photoshop and the other for Lightroom. If you wanted to use any other photo editing programs on your computer, you had to install further copies of the plug-in.

With Viveza 2.0, Nik has improved support the plug-in provides for the different software and programs you could use. Right off the bat, you get support for three different products, covering the entire Photoshop and Lightroom range you could use. For that, you have to follow the installation wizard and let it do its thing.

Speaking of support, Viveza 2 provides support for 64-bit photos as well which is a step up from the previous version of the plug-in. This is what makes installation and using the plug-in so much easier. You get support for 32-bit and 64-bit Photoshop and Lightroom from the start.

## Using Levels & Curves

One of the things learned from using the Viveza 2 plug-in for a while is that some adjustments are better left for the very end of the process. This is the case with the Levels & Curves adjustment. You have to apply it once you have adjusted all the other sliders that you needed to tweak.

The reason for this is that this adjustment changes the color tone of the image you are editing. Unless you have all the other image properties finalized, it could be difficult for you to figure out the best tone for your image. This is when using Levels & Curves wouldn't be such a good idea.

Expert Tips

One thing you should keep in mind is that this adjustment is available to you through Lightroom and Photoshop as well. However, using the main program to render this change will mean that you have to make the adjustments twice. First you will have to edit the image using the Viveza 2 plug-in and then adjust the Levels & Curves using Photoshop or Lightroom.

Same goes for all other adjustments in Viveza 2 that are available to you in Aperture, Lightroom and Photoshop. If you use them before you edit the image in Viveza, it would make it a two-step process for you. There is no need for you to forgo using the adjustments in Viveza 2 given that Nik has introduced them this time around.

Coming back to the point, you have to use Levels & Curves wisely as changing it would mean making changes to the entire image. You need to be careful with all the Global Adjustments that are available to you in Viveza 2 but most importantly, Levels & Curves.

These are some expert tips that will help you improve your user experience and get the best out of Viveza 2. As you can see, there are some tricks you can use to save money on buying the plug-in as well as making it easier for you to install it properly. There is no reason why you shouldn't follow these tips.

# CONCLUSION

This brings us to the end of our book on Viveza 2. As stated at the beginning, this book has covered the entire process of using the plug-in, from installation to editing the images. We have tried to be as comprehensive as possible, banking on our own experience of using the plug-in as well as some helpful and authentic resources.

Though this book is not a substitute for professional advice, you can use it as a guide to master the use of the great photo editing plug-in, Viveza 2. Reading this book from cover to cover will help you understand all that you need to know about the plug-in.

It is extremely important that you follow each and every step on the way. Otherwise, you might end up missing some important detail. It is the work that will suffer and you won't be able to get the image quality that you desire. This is why we would recommend that you read this book from start to finish before starting to use the plug-in.

There is little doubt that Viveza 2 is one of the best photo-editing plug-ins available on the market today. However, you need to make sure you are using it in the best way possible to make the most of it. This book is our humble attempt to help you do so.

Best of luck!